M Natalie McVeigh
   Apt 102
   770 N Grant St
   Denver, CO 80203

Don't Retire: Reinvent

Through the Meaningful Future™ Process

By Doug McPherson

Copyright © 2014 by Doug McPherson

All rights reserved
No part of this book maybe used or reproduced
in any manner whatsoever without written permission of the author.

Printed in the United States of America

ISBN 978-1502437518

Easy Read Publishers
4000 E. Bristol Street, Suite 3
Elkhart, IN 46514

*Don't know what life is going to be like
AFTER
you leave your company?*

> **REVEALED** FOR THE FIRST TIME EVER...
> THE WORLD'S ONLY SYSTEM FOR
> REINVENTING YOUR SELF
> **FOR THE REST OF YOUR LIFE!**

"How to Make Life AFTER You Leave Your Company the Best, Most Meaningful Years of Your Life!"

Dedication

To my clients, who for over 40 years have
allowed me to help them
create plans for their business succession
and a Meaningful Future™.

I am honored to have had a small
part in their lives.

Table of Contents

Introduction
Never Retire 1

CHAPTER 1
You're Not Going to Live Forever 9

CHAPTER 2
Who I Am and Why I Wrote This Book 17

CHAPTER 3
Harsh Reality: This Book is NOT For Everyone 29

CHAPTER 4
Doug McPherson Tells All His Meaningful Future Secrets.. 33

CHAPTER 5
Next Steps.. 73

APPENDIX Bucket List Ideas
Community/Giving 79

Travel 81

Technology 89

Sports and Fitness 89

Spiritual 91

Social/Food related 92

Out of the ordinary 93

Family/Legacy 99

Don't Retire: Reinvent through a Meaningful Future Process

Introduction

Never Retire

Welcome to what I sincerely hope is the most truthful, blunt, straightforward, non-sugarcoated, no-holds-barred book ever written on the subject of scrapping the idea of retirement and instead redefining and reinventing your remaining years to make them THE MOST MEANINGFUL of your entire life.

Let's face it. We're all getting older, and someday you'll have to hang up the day-to-day running of your business and redefine how you're going to spend whatever years you still have left.

You're going to have to take a long, hard look at where you are and where you want to go. Believe me, I know it's not easy — but it is possible with a bit of guidance.

I hope this book strikes a chord with you: the chord of authenticity.

Let's talk about what you WON'T find here.

This book WON'T rehash industry-taught retirement nonsense, only real-world truth from a guy who's been working with business owners in succession planning and defining their Meaningful Futures for over 40 years.

You also won't find any illusions here. I have written this book with the idea that you're having a private consultation with me. If we're sitting across from each other, I'll be telling you to lose the illusion about retiring and redefine your "talk track" to cover how the final years of your life will be the most meaningful.

And they CAN be, you know.

Yes, you won't be going into the office every day at the same time.

Yes, someone else will be managing the day-to-day of the business you spent so many years building.

And yes, it might even mean selling your business.

But when all is said and done, and we've gone through this well-defined process, the light will go on, clarity will reign, and you'll get excited about what the future holds. You'll find yourself looking forward to waking up every day, with a new zest for each morning you have.

Life will be fun again.

Isn't THAT worth ridding yourself of all the nonsense about "retirement"?

If you're reading this book, I think I already know something about you. I've learned a lot of things working with successful business owners. They want a well-defined plan, with specific steps, and a timetable to make it happen.

You want that, too.

You are goal-oriented.

So don't panic. In essence, your life after running your business (notice I am not saying "your life during your retirement years") shouldn't be any different in a lot of key ways.

How do you get THERE from HERE?

In this book you're going to learn:

- How to create and implement a **game plan** guaranteed to make the last years of your life the best they can be.

- How to ensure that there will never come a day after you leave your company that you won't have something **fulfilling, rewarding,** and **FUN** to do!

- How to **make sure your wife/husband doesn't get sick of you**, while still being around one another enough to enjoy quality time together.

- How to so drastically **REINVENT YOURSELF** that your kids brag to others about your **newfound life** (instead of being "worried about Dad/Mom")

- How to make your friends, former employees, and business associates JEALOUS when they see how much you're obviously **loving** your new life.

- How to leave an **incredible legacy** with more than just your business experience — with a whole new exciting chapter you've yet to live!

That's a tall order in such a small book. But this is your LIFE we're talking about. It deserves big plans and tall orders.

So what's your reaction to all this?

Wondering if this is all too good to be true?

Instinctively wanting to reject the possibility of a Meaningful Future?

Resisting the thought of walking away from your business?

Finding it hard to believe the idea that life

could be fun and exciting outside your business?

You're not alone. That's what makes what I do so much fun: when the light goes on and people believe this…it's priceless.

All I ask is that you hang in here with me. Let me prove to you that there really is life after business, and the future can be full of meaning.

I hope you profit greatly from our relationship. I welcome your comments, thoughts, or questions. You can communicate with me directly by email at:

doug@meaningfulfuture.com

Doug McPherson

CHAPTER 1

You're Not Going to Live Forever

Let's face it. We're all getting older, and someday you'll have to hang up the day-to-day running of your business and redefine how you're going to spend whatever years you still have left.

We all know the only things sure in this life are death and taxes, and yet most of my clients bury their heads in the sand and act like they'll live forever.

…Except when it comes to their finances.

I have found most higher-wealth people have spent a great deal of time working on their financial plan and are quite set for their retirement years. For these people, dealing with the money isn't the problem.

The problem I'm talking about is everyday living.

Having fun.

Doing something meaningful beyond just working.

Leaving a legacy.

Defining who you are in the last 15 years of your life.

Statistics show that the average person in the U.S. lives to be 83 years old. That means if you are 64 years old or older, you likely have somewhere around 15-20 years left, give or take a few years.

You're in what I call the "Red Zone."

Just like in football, the Red Zone means you've worked hard to get the ball 80 percent down the field, and now you're 20 yards from the end zone.

And yet we find most business owners have focused ALL of their time and energy to the first 80 percent of their lives, and given virtually NO thought to how they're going to spend the final 20 percent of their lives!

Are You In or Close to The Red Zone? Then It's Time to GET BUSY.

Just for fun, think back with me about 15 years, to the year 1999.

```
In 1999...
  • Dow Jones went over 10,000 for
    the first time, and two months
    later hit 11,000.
  • The Euro was introduced.
  • Former pro wrestler Jesse
    Ventura was sworn in as governor
    of Minnesota.
  • President Clinton began his
    impeachment trial in the Senate
    and was later acquitted.
  • Michael Jordan announced his
    retirement, only to come back
    two years later
  • The Columbine High School
    massacre left 13 dead.
```

Remember these events? They don't seem that long ago, do they?

As you can see, 15 years isn't a long time.

You've lived 80 percent of your life already. Only 20 percent more to go — not a lot of time to do those things that you've always wanted to do but just never got around to doing because you've been busy building your business.

But what if time isn't the problem?

Maybe you don't really want to have all that time on your hands…because you don't have any earthly idea what you're going to do when you stop coming into the office. It's all you've ever known your whole life, and now the thought of NOT doing it scares the hell out of you.

Sound familiar?

You're not alone. In fact, the MAJORITY of my clients feel this way. And it's for this very reason I wrote this book and why I created The Meaningful Future Process. I'll introduce the process later, but first I should share with you who I am and why I wrote this book.

> **Did You Know that the "Challenge of Retirement" is greater for successful business owners and executives…**
>
> ```
> Successful business owners and executives
> often face a more profound sense of loss
> than the average retiree.
>
> New retirees do not experience a sense of
> loss during the exciting "honeymoon" phase
> of a new retirement.  It eventually may
> appear in symptoms of discontent,
> irritability and depression.
>
> Successful business people who take the
> traditional path of retirement find
> themselves surrendering, abruptly in many
> cases, tremendous amounts of POWER and
> DAILY STRATEGIC PROBLEM SOLVING that had
> been their habit for decades.
> ```

Don't Retire: Reinvent through a Meaningful Future Process

Running their business was not only a lot more than a JOB, it was much more than a CAREER, too. In fact, it was the most important aspect of their life. It was their sense of purpose and identity.

Many business owners "in retirement" often cannot identify or understand exactly why their life seems to be getting progressively less and less enjoyable.

In fact, their overall unease and sense of restlessness is due to the lack of meaning in their life. They no longer know where their TRUCK is going!

Powerful, successful business owners are often more prone to struggle emotionally in retirement, since, in a way, they are giving up more. They have to adjust to a greater reduction in levels of daily intensity, strategic interaction and critical thinking than the average retiree.

Ultimately, many may find a sense of satisfaction and well-being after they redirect or "re-purpose" their higher intellect towards a new, meaningful and intellectually challenging strategic cause.

CHAPTER 2
Who I Am and Why I Wrote This Book

My name is Doug McPherson, and I've worked exclusively with construction and aggregate industry business owners for over 41 years, helping them with their financial and succession plans. How did I get here?

I started out to be your typical financial planner.

It was in the early '70s and just like today, there was a lot of competition. A wise mentor of mine once told me that riches were in the niches, so I began to look for specific industries and owners to whom I could relate strongly.

Those business niches turned out to be construction and aggregate. I could relate to their methodical ways of looking at things.

They had blueprints, timelines, and focus on a specific goal.

> *"When I think about leaving this all behind and venturing off into <u>unknown territory</u>, I have to admit, I'm not thrilled with the idea. But instead of avoiding the topic or being paralyzed by fear of change, instead I decided to EMBRACE the inevitable."*
>
> Doug McPherson

That made sense to me.

But what I soon found out was that most of them already had a planner they trusted to manage their financial portfolio. No surprise there: if your work life is based on blueprints, plans, and specific milestones, you're likely to apply the same approach to your finances.

So, rather than compete, I decided to specialize in succession planning and developed what I call The McPherson® Critical Path Process.™ No one else was doing anything like that, so I became the "go-to expert."

Through this niche, I became so involved with my clients that…

- I'm a long-standing member of 7 national construction associations.

- I helped develop the prominent Construction Financial Management Association (CFMA) Washington, D.C. Chapter.
- I've been a featured speaker at numerous national conventions of various construction associations.
- I've produced articles published in various publications by McGraw-Hill.
- And, for 17 years, I co-sponsored the very popular one-week "Ski Seminar" in Aspen, Telluride, and Vail, regularly attended by many of the most influential people in the industry

You see, I'm "one of you." I've been in this industry my whole life.

Almost all my clients are construction or aggregate company owners.

And it's not just my affiliation with this industry that gives me unique insight into the challenges you're facing with the transition out of your company.

There's another thing we have in common:

I'm in my retirement years.

Everything that I'm going to share with you in this book is written for me as much as it is for you.

All of the proven concepts and processes we've built into the Meaningful Future Process came from the key question I struggled with as I came face-to-face with my own mortality:

What am I going to do with the final years of my life here on Planet Earth?

Don't get me wrong. I love my work.

I love the people I get to work with every day; my clients, my employees (my assistant Jan has been with me for over 32 years!), vendors, business associates, industry connections — these are the people I've spent the lion's share of my life with.

But, just like you, how am I going to feel when they're not around anymore?

I still find my work interesting and challenging. And because I've been doing it so long, I'm really good at it!

When I go into a new succession or estate plan transaction, that longevity is one huge advantage that my competitors can't claim. When you've been doing something for 40 plus years, there's hardly any issue or problem that arises that you haven't already seen; you're not "reinventing the wheel."

I know how to "get 'er done" eight ways to Sunday!

So it seems a shame to just walk away from it all.

This is my world.

I've created it.

I'm comfortable here.

When I think about leaving this all behind and venturing off into unknown territory, I have to admit, I'm not thrilled with the idea.

(Sounds familiar, doesn't it?)

But instead of avoiding the topic or being paralyzed by fear of change, I decided to EMBRACE the inevitable.

Truth is, I have 15 or so years left on this Earth, so I've decided to be INTENTIONAL about making sure these years are the very best they can be.

When I meet privately with my clients, they tell me the same thing. They're very concerned.

Chances are good if you're reading this, you've built a very successful company, maybe multiple companies.

You've made a lot of money.

You've traveled.

Don't Retire: Reinvent through a Meaningful Future Process

You have all the toys and trophies to show for it.

You've worked very, very hard your whole life, and as a result your family, employees, clients, and community have all benefited.

But now it's time to move on and let someone else take over — maybe your sons, key employees, or a possible purchaser.

When My Clients Finally Leave Their Companies, They Ask Me...
"Doug, What Am I Supposed To Do *NOW?*"

I wrote this book to give you a roadmap to your Meaningful Future. If I've done my job, what you are about to read is going to (at least momentarily)…double or triple your heart rate.

Why?

Because for the first time I honestly believe

I have cracked the code on living the last 20 percent of your life to the fullest

I am going to tell you right up front that this is NOT some "fluke" that has worked with just one or two selected people out there. It's taken me years and years to perfect the system with my high-net-worth clients.

Why would I share my secrets in this small book that costs less than a single meal at a nice restaurant?

Let me answer that by telling you a story....

A client's wife called me one day in tears. Her 47-year marriage was on the line. While she had her own business and hobbies, her newly-retired husband was completely lost.

"You need to reinvent my husband — not retire him," she told me. "If you don't, we'll be divorced within the year."

It was then I realized retirement without reinvention is almost guaranteed to fail. Once the business side of things has been settled, there's got to be a really good answer to that question, "What NOW?" An answer that's meaningful, and INTENTIONAL.

I knew then I had to create the Meaningful Future Process. And that's what I set out to do.

CHAPTER 3
Harsh Reality: This Book is NOT For Everyone

I think it's important to take a few minutes and talk about whom this book is NOT for — to find out if you should just close it up now and get back to work or…if by some small glimmer of light…I might just have something of significant value that you should stop and pay attention to.

First, let's get a few things straight, right out of the gate:

1. This is NOT a book for business owners who refuse to face the fact that they're not going to live forever and simply say they're going to work until they die.

It is not my job to beat you over the head with a 2-by-4 and get you to "wake up." If you don't want a Meaningful Future, I can't make you want it. What I can promise is that if you'll pause for a moment and give me just a small amount of your attention, you might find out the last 15 years or so of your life can be really GREAT.

2. This book is NOT for family members to read and shove down the business owner's throat.

I encourage all family members to read this book also. To know what the Meaningful Future really is — not something they dream up in their head. But just because you read about it doesn't give you the right to "decide" that someone else needs this…and harangue them about it!

On the other hand, we encourage the spouse to go through the process after yours is finished or in some cases at the same time. Even though each Meaningful Future will be unique to you, your futures will also be tied together.

3. **This book is NOT for a business owner who is "too busy" to take the process seriously; anything worthwhile takes time.**

And defining and planning for your Meaningful Future is no exception. If you can't carve out a few hours a week to focus, then I can't help you. There will be things you'll have to think about, write down, and spend time discussing with me. I can only help you along the process, but I can't do it for you.

If you've got any of these issues working, we'll need to deal with them before you can do the work required for your Meaningful Future. But if you can honestly say none of those things will be a problem…you're cleared for takeoff.

Let's get started!

CHAPTER 4

Doug McPherson Tells All His Meaningful Future Secrets

As I as stated in the introduction of this book, I have usually been described as a no-nonsense, truthful succession planner. These people would be correct in describing me as a person who does not believe in confusing fantasy with reality. Worth saying again is that, in fact, I believe in "accurate thinking" over positive thinking and have found I am most successful when I have a firm grip on the way things really are and least successful when caught wrestling with the way things "ought to be."

So let's remember where we are, with no sugarcoating: If you're reading this book right now, you probably have no more than 15-20 years left to your life. You don't have a minute more to waste!

That's why…

The goal of The Meaningful Future Process is NOT to "retire" you.

It's to REINVENT you.

That may be a new term to you, and it doesn't help that it means different things to different people. Many people "reinvent" themselves numerous times over their lives — going into totally different careers, changing the direction and focus of what they do, giving up some things and bringing others in.

What we're talking about here, however, is the period of time in a business owner's life when they no longer go to the office on a daily basis. Here's a story you might relate to:

> **Former Unmotivated, Succession-Stalling CEO Gets REINVENTED To Become Busy Real Estate Development Consultant**
>
> *One of my well-known site contractor clients was having a very hard time with his management succession plan. Even though he had three sons and talented key people in the company, he simply couldn't imagine not coming to work every day like he had done for the last 55 years since he started the company.*
>
> *Of course, he knew that the company couldn't continue without a management*

succession component going forward at some point, but due to concerns about his own future, he was simply stalling the process. Not only did his stalling begin to affect the morale of the management team; the surety and banking people were starting to become very concerned as well. But since he wasn't motivated by what the future had in store for him, he was impeding the future success of his company, and he knew it.

As part of The Meaningful Future Process, we discovered he had an interest in developing some real estate investments that he owned. We then helped him develop meaningful long-term goals in relation to those interests and created a step-by-step critical path to achieve those goals. We set up a number of other operating LLCs and structured some formal relationships with a number of developers for whom he was already doing some consulting work. The result: The real estate development projects have become very lucrative and have kept him very busy, taking his focus almost completely away from the day-to-day activities of his

Don't Retire: Reinvent through a Meaningful Future Process

> ```
> company. This has enabled his talented
> sons to step forward and manage it,
> where they are doing a great job.
> ```

For REINVENTION to work, it must involve something compelling: just thinking about it excites and interests you.

To some, the story above may sound like my client left one job on one day and clocked into another job the next — not their idea of "fun."

This means that reinvention is more than just finding a new way to do what you're already doing. That can be part of another "reinvention" process…but that's not what we're talking about here.

We're talking about different — and compelling.

You're probably not "excited" about coming to work every day and doing the same thing you've been doing for the last 40+ years, but at least you're comfortable. You may find it "compelling," but only in the sense that you don't have anything else to put your hand to — at least nothing you know will be better.

So you stay in that comfort rut, because "the devil I know is better than the devil I don't know."

But that's no way to truly LIVE the rest of your life.

The only thing that's going to motivate you OUT of that "comfort zone" is something that captures your imagination: a vision of what a "future you" COULD look like that you find exciting, dynamic, and — most of all — motivating enough to take the steps required to make it happen.

For the client above, it meant REINVENTING himself from a business standpoint.

He couldn't see his "future self" as someone one who didn't work at all. He just needed to work on something else that he personally found meaningful and rewarding.

Now, that's not for everyone.

Not everyone wants to just "find another job" or "find different work."

Not everyone wants to "work" as hard in their reinventions as they are in their present companies!

But once they've reinvented themselves, people may find that the "work" they do doesn't feel like WORK at all.

Like this client:

> ### Altruistic Executive Finds a Way to "Pay It Forward."
>
> ```
> So many of my clients have no clue
> what "life" is like without "work"
> that they're in a panic at the
> thought of not going into that
> workplace every day. One of my
> clients had it all: he'd won
> Businessperson of the Year, he'd
> served on several charitable boards,
> and he'd put three kids through
> college, and he still looked forward
> to the next challenge every day.
> And, even more than most, he was a
> no-nonsense guy; he didn't believe
> in a lot of "self-actualization
> mumbo-jumbo," as he put it. A self-
> made man, he didn't waste time
> analyzing success; he just made it
> happen.
> ```

Don't Retire: Reinvent through a Meaningful Future Process

So when he first encountered the Meaningful Future Process, at first he was resistant; he didn't want to spend time "navel gazing," he just wanted to "get on with it." Finally, he gave in and made a bucket List, to discover it heavily weighted in terms of "paying it forward": building houses for Habitat for Humanity, supplying a local food bank, advocacy for the needy, and the like. He was grateful for the opportunities he'd had, and once he saw that the rest of his life could be about helping others have the same chances, he got so excited it was impossible to stop him.

Now, although the rest of his community considers him "retired," he knows he's actually "reinvented" and having a ball matching community organizations with members of his circle who want to "pay it forward" in ways that really make a difference. He doesn't miss his former "workplace" one bit; interestingly enough, his company's doing better than ever with all the positive PR that's come from his

> particular approach to a Meaningful Future.

This is just one example of how "reinventing" can also bring benefits to the business you've left behind! Not a bad deal!

So it's not about just finding new "work" to do. That's not what many people want.

Not everyone wants to WORK…They just don't want to be BORED. And once they're not BORED anymore, amazing things can happen to everybody around them.

Remember, the REINVENTION process is different for everyone. Here's a real-life story of another client who took a very different route:

Former Electrical Contractor Sells Company and Starts New Life as Farmer/Boater/Travel Enthusiast

One of my successful electrical contractor clients hem-hawed around for years without knowing what he should do with his company. For a long time **it seemed he would just "keep on keeping on"**.

But after going through the Meaningful Future™ exercises in great detail with him, we finally discovered some **things he always wanted to do** but never figured he would have the time. It turned out that time was not the issue - a plan was. Once we created the **step-by-step PLAN to make happen**, his whole attitude - and life - changed.

We helped him make his Meaningful Future a reality, and it was decided the first step was for him to sell his company. We helped him sell for $22M, so now he has plenty of money in the bank to do what he wants to do for the rest of his life. He's now doing a lot of farming, plus he has a big boat that he uses to travel around a lot on the east coast.

```
He goes to Nova Scotia certain times
of the year and goes to the
Caribbean in the winter. He is a
real happy guy.
```

As you can see, this client wasn't that keyed up about continuing to "work." He just wanted to make darn sure he had something interesting and meaningful to DO during the time he has left on this Earth. Sometimes "work" needs to be redefined.

How to REINVENT Yourself Instead of Retiring

So how do you make your OWN successful "reinvention" story?

The Meaningful Future Process.

The Meaningful Future Process is a proprietary 8-step process I developed specifically for business owners in their fifties, sixties, and seventies. That doesn't mean someone younger or older can't take advantage of developing a plan for their future, but it is critical that those over fifty start the process.

Now, my clients are very visually oriented. They're used to looking at blueprints and timelines, so I designed the Meaningful Future Process to be step-by-step.

But you don't have to be a "visual" person, let alone in construction, to use this process. Step-by-step instructions work for all of us.

In this chapter, I'm going to go through each step with you so you can see how the process works.

Step #1 – Define your current situation

It's a fact that 99.9 percent of business owners never stop long enough to think about where they are and where they want to go. They are hard-charging, working on today's project and the next deal.

But to have the last 15-20 years of your life become the most meaningful, it is critical to stop and think.

To plan.

To timeline.

To prioritize.

To imagine what life could be like.

And I start the process with a scorecard, an honest assessment of where you are at this very moment in time. It's a simple 10-question scorecard, but when we work together, it tells me a lot about your current situation.

Don't Retire: Reinvent through a Meaningful Future Process

 THE MEANINGFUL FUTURE SCORECARD℠

SCORE
YOUR CURRENT SITUATION ON A SCALE OF 1-10. RECORD YOUR REACTIONS TO THESE MEANINGFUL FUTURE ELEMENTS.

WORST	1	2	3	4	5	6	7	8	9	10	BEST
I DO NOT HAVE A VISION FOR A MEANINGFUL FUTURE.											I HAVE A WRITTEN VISION FOR MY MEANINGFUL FUTURE.
I DO NOT HAVE A PLAN FOR MY LIFE BEYOND MY BUSINESS.											I HAVE A CLEAR PLAN FOR MY LIFE BEYOND MY BUSINESS.
I AM CONCERNED ABOUT MY FINANCIAL FUTURE.											I AM CLEAR AND CONFIDENT ABOUT MY FINANCIAL FUTURE.
I DO NOT TAKE THE TIME TO REFLECT DEEPLY ABOUT WHAT I REALLY WANT TO DO WITH THE REST OF MY LIFE.											I REGULARLY TAKE TIME TO REFLECT DEEPLY ABOUT WHAT I WANT TO DO WITH THE REST OF MY LIFE.
I DO NOT KNOW WHAT CONTRIBUTION I WANT TO MAKE OR LEGACY I WANT TO LEAVE.											I AM CLEAR ABOUT WHAT CONTRIBUTION I WANT TO MAKE AND WHAT LEGACY I WANT TO LEAVE.
I HAVE NOT PROPERLY COMMUNICATED MY VALUES TO MY FAMILY AND SUCCESSORS FOR THE FUTURE.											I HAVE CREATED LETTERS OF DIRECTION FOR MY FAMILY AND MANAGEMENT LEGACY WORKSHEET FOR MY SUCCESSORS.
I FEEL STRESSED AND CONCERNED ABOUT THE FUTURE OF MY BUSINESS.											I AM CONFIDENT AND PLEASED ABOUT THE FUTURE OF MY BUSINESS.
OUR MANAGEMENT SUCCESSION PLAN IS UNFOCUSED AND INCOMPLETE.											OUR MANAGEMENT SUCCESSION PLAN IS DEFINED AND IN WRITING.
OUR COMPANY'S EQUITY SUCCESSION PLAN IS UNCLEAR.											OUR COMPANY'S EQUITY SUCCESSION PLAN IS DEFINED AND IN WRITING.
I DO NOT HAVE ANYONE HELPING ME ACHIEVE MY MEANINGFUL FUTURE.											I HAVE A TRUSTED ADVISOR HELPING ME ACHIEVE MY MEANINGFUL FUTURE.

TO SPEAK WITH DOUG McPHERSON ABOUT YOUR MEANINGFUL FUTURE SCORECARD℠ RESULTS, PLEASE CALL 703-879-2581 OR EMAIL DOUG AT doug@meaningfulfuture.com

Don't worry if you get a low score. That's normal. In fact, if you get a high score, you are a very rare person indeed.

Truth is, most of my clients have scored low. And it doesn't matter how "big" they are.

I've sat across the desk from men with net worth in excess of $500 million and they've not had good answers to these questions! Why is that? Well, chances are good nobody has ever "talked straight" and helped them confront these tough questions head-on.

The good news is, this is just the beginning of The Meaningful Future Process.

The objective with the process isn't just to "root out" the bad without giving you a solution. No way! The goal is to ask the tough questions and give you an honest "score," but more importantly, it's to give you a visual, sequential, and time-lined process to turn that score from wherever you are now into "all 10's."

Because when you are honestly able to say you score all 10's, you will have REINVENTED your LIFE.

But it is important to do this step. You can't skip it or brush it off, or the entire process will fall apart.

Part of Step 1: The Bucket List

Believe it or not, you are a prime candidate for composing a bucket list. You're successful. Focused. An action-taker.

What's in a bucket list?

That depends.

It doesn't have to be an all-consuming race against time, like the 2007 *Bucket List* movie (directed by Rob Reiner and starring Jack Nicholson and Morgan Freeman).

It could be a leisurely endeavor that, coincidentally enough, involves trying to develop a succession plan.

A bucket list can give you a reason to get up in the morning.

Why would you need this? Well…

Some people want to remain in bed because they feel they have no worlds left to conquer; others cower there because they feel no one cares whether they live or die. A bucket list provides new challenges for the former and a cheering section for the latter.

A bucket list can give answers to some of life's most depressing questions and help you rise above despair. When you find yourself sighing, "Where did the years go?" you can look with pride upon your trophies, certificates, photo albums, memorabilia, and collectibles shelf and find assurance that you haven't just wasted your opportunities. You made your days matter.

> My Meaningful Future
> → Sell company vs turn over to my sons
> What I'd like to do
> By Rudays
> * Play poker game with high rollers
> * Tango with wife in Argentina
> * Go fire walking
> * Have a street named after me
> * Have a beer at Oktoberfest in Germany
> * Donate $1 million. Create a foundation to handle
> * Play golf in all top golf places
> * Sky dive
> * Race on a Nascar track
>
> Grow my real estate holdings
>
> 4 Travel
> 4 Hobbies
> 4 Vacation

"Why am I here?"

"What is the meaning of life?"

Working on a bucket list does not come with a money-back guarantee that you will answer those questions, but the odds of success are certainly greater when you're out there stretching yourself and facing the world instead of huddling in your comfort zone.

A bucket list can bring order to chaos.

A bucket list lets you leave a legacy for your descendants. You won't be just a tombstone with a birth date and a death date. When family stories are swapped, you'll be revered as the great-grandpa or great-grandma who excelled by breaking a record at the Paralympics or brainstorming a revolutionary method of recycling or learning to play the piano at age 86.

A bucket list hands you the perfect opportunity to do an honest, objective analysis of your physical/mental/emotional strengths, weaknesses, and limitations.

Perhaps you will find that public speaking really isn't so bad, or that you really can improve your memory skills. On the other hand, the final analysis may show that you really do have a lousy sense of direction, or that you will always be nauseous around blood. So, in the future, you can confidently volunteer to purchase all the supplies for a party or serve as master of ceremonies — and abstain without guilt when asked to travel to the far side of town for a blood drive.

Obviously, a quest for a bucket list can bring

you many new friends and acquaintances. Those who help you and admire you as you show the gumption to work through the challenges on it may stick with you for a lifetime.

Here are some categories for you to think about when developing your bucket list:

- Community/Giving
- Travel
- Technology
- Sports and Fitness
- Spiritual
- Social
- Out of the ordinary
- Family/Legacy

Bucket lists can be anything. Even crazy things like:

✓ Anonymously **foot the bill** for a young or elderly restaurant

- ✓ customer who seems out of his league.
- ✓ Learn to **Tango in Argentina**.
- ✓ **Stand** on the shoulders of giants, by reading a biography and replicating an early accomplishment by one of your idols.
- ✓ **Follow the Yellow Brick Road** by building your own scarecrow, by searching for ruby slippers, or by finally getting an appraisal of all those gold items lying around the house.
- ✓ **Toe the line** by subjecting yourself to fat camp, a dude ranch, or some other environment that will discipline you.
- ✓ **Run with the bulls** at Pamplona, Spain — or a local ranch or stockyard.
- ✓ **Saunter** into an Old West saloon and have an old-timey picture made of you drinking your first sarsaparilla.
- ✓ **Walk the line** by seeing how long you can dress in black — like The Man in Black, Johnny Cash.

- ✓ **Hop on board** a train, subway, horse-drawn buggy, airplane,
- ✓ riverboat, UFO, or whatever conveyance you've never ridden before.
- ✓ Do the **Walk of Life** by helping with a charity event for others in dire straits.
- ✓ Learn more about wildlife. Even if you're not a hunter, buy some seed and fertilizer and **start a food plot to attract deer.**
- ✓ In the spirit of *Reader's Digest*, **make an album with photos** and anecdotes of the biggest, most colorful "characters" you've ever encountered.
- ✓ **Write a book.**
- ✓ Seek out some guys who are "well-thumbed" and cheer for them at a **thumb-wrestling** competition.
- ✓ Save bits and pieces of old clocks. Use the collected parts to **build a clock from scratch.**
- ✓ Learn to **churn your own butter** for your own use.
- ✓ Become "the voice" of your favorite charity or nonprofit organization by recording **public service announcements.**

- ✓ **Help a company** reorganize under the Chapter 11 bankruptcy rules.
- ✓ **Mentor** a young person.
- ✓ Enter to win a **cooking contest** with your fanciest onion soup.
- ✓ Go exploring the **Continental Shelf**.
- ✓ Drive the entire **Route 66**.
- ✓ Develop a really exciting narrative about what you do on weekends by working with the **hook-and-ladder crew** of the volunteer fire department.
- ✓ Learn the history of "America's Pastime" as it was at the turn of the last century with **Old Time Baseball Players** in your area.
- ✓ Spend a whole year **traveling the world in an RV** and **learn how to blog about it**. Pick one subject for the trip, like reviewing a locally-owned restaurant in the cities you visit.

As you can see, such a list could be endless, but I think you get the idea. The important thing is to take action.

Instead of storing these ideas in your head, start your bucket list now. In the Appendix at the back of this book I've given you some bucket list idea starters. Certainly the list could be much larger, but it's a point to start from.

Put down every dream you've ever had. It doesn't matter if they seem "silly." It doesn't matter if they seem impossible. This is a bucket list, remember?

If you've always dreamed of doing it, put it there. We've got time for sorting later. When you and I meet to go over your Meaningful Future Process, we will begin to explore your dreams and bucket lists to identify the ones most important to you. We'll set priorities and eventually structure a timeline.

Steps #2 to #5 – Visioning and Goal Setting

My objective in this phase is for you to clearly see your future.

What does it look like?

How does it feel?

What happens when you're not going to work anymore?

Whom are you spending time with?

What time do you get up in the morning and what does your calendar look like?

How involved (if any) are you still in your old business? Do you still want to see the financials? Or have you moved on?

Keep in mind, there are no "right" or "wrong" answers here — except that we're not letting the word "retire" enter into the proceedings! But this is an exploring phase. Take advantage of it to probe to find what you REALLY want.

And yes, it takes time. But it's worth the time to do, because it will pay dividends beyond any ordinary "retirement" plan you'll find.

One caveat.

We may be putting the cart before the horse here, though, in asking about details…until we determine WHY you're doing these things. WHY the specific items on your bucket list are important…and WHY they speak to you.

If the "why" is strong enough, the "how" will follow. Just know that you need to know the WHY, or the list may be just a nice idea — but not something that gets you excited enough to "plug into."

So....

Why should you have a Meaningful Future?

Who besides yourself benefits?

Why do you want each item on your bucket list?

The answers may surprise you.

If they do, that's good.

If they rattle you a little, that's even better. Because change doesn't happen until your "cage" gets rattled a bit.

That's what this kind of exploring will do. And, again, it'll pay dividends beyond what you'll ever expect.

If you've been in a particularly comfortable "rut," it may get you excited and enthused about your life for the first time in a long time.

Then, we'll talk about what keeps you from doing those things on the bucket list, and in your Meaningful Future, already.

In this phase of the process, it's all about my asking a lot of questions and helping you figure out what obstacles could be preventing you from moving on.

Obstacles are identified and resolved.

Options are identified and quantified.

And THEN….magic happens. I've never seen it to fail, and it's a kick every time.
It starts to become clear to you.

What a Meaningful Future really means to YOU, your spouse, your family. All the people in your life.

And yes, it DOES affect everyone in your life. Everyone in your little corner of the universe.

You see, up to now I've been talking primarily to you only, but in reality, couples do this process simultaneously. And that's a good thing.

Don't underestimate either the importance of this or its value. Your "sweetie" can often provide valuable input and help — and since your spouse has to live with the results, it's crucial to include him/her in how you get there!

Steps #6 to #8 – Implementation

By this time in the process, my clients are really getting excited. They have a vision and well-defined goals. Now all they have to do is put the specific plan together and arrive at a timeline to make it happen.

This is where you'll design what I call the Meaningful Future Critical Path.

Many of you are already familiar with

the term "critical path" through the field of project management. For those of you who aren't, here's a thumbnail explanation and application.

A Critical Path talks about four key elements:

- A list of activities that have to be accomplished to complete a project. For our purposes, that list will entail the plan by which you exit your company and enter your Meaningful Future, whatever that looks like.

- The timeline and priority level for each activity that has been selected for action.

- How the activities are interdependent—in other words,

which step depends on other steps in order to get done.

- The logical end point. In business, that's a deliverable or a milestone. In your Meaningful Future Process, that's your desired outcome for the next 15-20 years, and how it's going to happen.

Using these guides, you can then calculate the appropriate path toward your Meaningful Future, and the earliest and latest each step can start and finish without delaying the project as a whole.

A key part of this is determining "critical" items—those which will take the longest—and which of the items have what's called "total float" and can be delayed without the project itself being delayed.

So the "critical path" for your Meaningful Future is the longest potential time it can take for all the steps to be accomplished to get you into that future. Ironically enough, this is the very LEAST amount of time you should expect the process to take.

We talk about three-year plans, five-year plans, and other timelines…but until you determine your Critical Path, you won't have a realistic idea of just how long to expect these things to take.

And if you're familiar with Murphy's Law, you know planning for the LONGEST amount of time is only common sense!

The good news is that once you DO, you're already on the way to making it happen.

But — surprise! — setting forth on the Critical Path is a TEAM SPORT.

You may never have played team sports before in your life. Congratulations! You're doing it now!

Because any good project manager knows that you can't get a project done without a great project TEAM. And the same goes for your Meaningful Future Process Critical Path.

So who's on YOUR team?

We already talked about your spouse or significant other. Put other family members in there, too; they're not only going to be affected by your plans but they can help you get them done.

Who else could be on your TEAM?

- Relatives

- Key employees. After all, they're the ones who'll be responsible for the company once you've stepped away!

- Financial planner

- Attorney

- Insurance broker

- Other professionals with whom you deal on an everyday or frequent basis

- Family business and/or family office consultants

- Anyone else who will be involved in or impacted by your plans

Only you can determine who needs to be on your team, but don't leave anyone out who may want to be there.

Conversely, however, don't feel you need to force anyone to join you. Being asked to be involved in this process is a privilege, but it shouldn't be a burden, either. Your plan is, at its heart, YOUR plan.

Although it just might inspire your team members to think about THEIR Meaningful Futures, too.

And in that case, your invitation can make a difference for THEIR lives.

Which is one of the greatest paybacks of ALL - Meaningful Futures for your family, your friends, your colleagues…talk about a great item to put on your bucket list!

So are you excited yet? Plan your work, work your plan, and have a Meaningful Future…it sure beats the same-ol' same-ol' alternative of being "retired" and "out to pasture," doesn't it?

I thought it would!

CHAPTER 5
Next Steps

Well, there you have it. My entire process from start to finish.

1. Assess your current situation using our assessment tools
2. Create your bucket list, timeline, and prioritize the items

3. Establish your three-year (and then your long-term) vision, goals, timeline & prioritize
4. Identify obstacles and strategies to overcome the obstacles
5. Design your Meaningful Future Critical Path
6. Build your Meaningful Future Team
7. Implement your Meaningful Future Critical Path

As you can imagine, there can be numerous things required to put those steps into action. There is no way I can anticipate every situation for everyone reading this book.

But what I can do is offer to spend 90 minutes with you to listen about your particular situation. The meeting is FREE. Don't worry: this isn't some kind of "hard-sales-pitch" *disguised* as a free consultation.

> ## During this FREE Private Meeting, we will:
>
> 1. **Discuss your Meaningful Future Scorecard:** we'll take a good, honest look at where you really stand
> 2. **Identify DANGERS:** we'll determine what's keeping you from REINVENTING yourself
> 3. **Identify OPPORTUNITIES:** we'll ascertain what holds the greatest promise for making the final phase of your life the happiest and most meaningful
> 4. **Identify KEY STRENGTHS:** we'll uncover strengths you possess that give you the greatest sense of satisfaction when you share them
> 5. **Your Bucket List:** we'll discuss what you want to do before you kick the bucket
> 6. **Mortality Reality Projector:** we'll calculate your potential life span

That being said, I'm so convinced that this FREE one-on-one meeting will absolutely change the way you look at the rest of your life, I will back it up with this Crazy Guarantee:

During our time together, I will go over

The Meaningful Future Process and any questions you have about it, with no obligation on your part whatsoever

But even if you decide the whole "package" isn't for you, the clarity and inspiration that you gain from this free meeting ALONE could be a MAJOR TURNING POINT in this pivotal time of your life.

Give me a call! You've got nothing to lose. And I can't wait to see what you GAIN.

Call me at 703-879-2581

Should I work this out for myself or should I hire someone to help me?

One of the things I do for my clients is to offer a *Confidentiality Agreement*. Not that I would ever use a client's name without his permission in ANY setting, or divulge private situations, but it gives everyone a sense of their boundaries. I've had clients tell me things that no one else knows, and I value their trust in me.

Also a person can work through the process on their own, but having someone to talk to, to emphasize certain areas, to clarify thoughts and issues can be very helpful and speed up the process by helping you focus your thoughts on the task at hand.

It is very easy to rush the hard parts in order to reach conclusions that would be different when thought through.

It is easy to misconstrue the point of a question or task and this can alter conclusions.

The presence of a trusted advisor who has worked through this process for themselves and their clients will help clarify the process for you and provide a roadmap to satisfactory results.

Any advisor that offers this process has gone through every step and had similar discussions with me and with their clients.

Are you (or is someone you know) interested in becoming a licensed Advisor of the Meaningful Future Program?

An exciting new way to grow your existing service related business!

As you have been reading this book, have you been thinking about some of your existing clients who could really benefit by completing The Meaningful Future Process℠? Would you like to really stand out from your competitors? If so, look into licensing The Meaningful Future Process℠.

This unique comprehensive process creates in-depth conversations with clients and prospects about what they want to do with the rest of their lives. These conversations can lead to a stronger client relationship whatever your particular line of business is. The materials we have developed for our clients have helped us stand out from other advisors. No-one we have met has ever encountered a powerful program like this one.

By creating a meaningful vision for their lives, our clients are more excited about their futures, and are more motivated about planning for it. The program emphasizes that successful business people have the tools to reinvent themselves, rather than simply retiring from their business. That is very empowering!

Based on our success using this program, we are now offering it to other advisors.

If you are interested in learning more about this opportunity, please visit our website, www.meaningfulfuture.com, call Doug at 703.879.2581 or email him at doug@meaningfulfuture.com

APPENDIX
Bucket List Ideas

Community/Giving

1. Volunteer at the local prison
2. Give away your things to younger people who need it
3. Find someone to whom you can teach a skill you have
4. Start a non-profit foundation to give away your wealth
5. Thank a war veteran every day for a year
6. Plant a tree in someone's memory
7. Buy food for a homeless person

8. Volunteer at a homeless shelter and not just during the holidays
9. Help sponsor an Olympic athlete
10. Volunteer at your local Special Olympics
11. Volunteer your time with a cause that uses your special talents
12. Contribute to a cause you believe in but have an actively supported
13. Donate your hair to charity
14. Donate blood
15. Become a bone marrow donor
16. Become an organ donor
17. Leave an outrageous tip for an overworked waiter or waitress every day for a year
18. Visit three people in a nursing home or hospital every week
19. Volunteer at a nursing home
20. Host a foreign exchange student
21. Teach someone to read

22. Mentor a child
23. Put together a jigsaw puzzle with a child
24. Sponsor a child in a developing country
25. Build a house with Habitat for Humanity
26. Serve in the Peace Corps
27. Adopt an endangered species

Travel

28. Travel cross country by train
29. Go on an archaeological dig
30. Climb Mount Everest
31. Go spelunking
32. Pan for gold
33. Stay in an ice hotel
34. Plan and take a round the world dream trip
35. Buy an RV and visit all 50 states

36. Watch Native American tribal dancers perform
37. Go to the circus
38. Attend a Star Wars convention
39. Dig for fossils
40. Tour a big newspaper printing plant
41. Take the polar bear plunge
42. Spend Christmas on the beach
43. Trade homes for two weeks with someone from another country
44. Fly a kite on the beach
45. Visit the rain forest
46. See a volcano
47. Visit Glacier National Park
48. Visit Yosemite National Park
49. Visit Yellowstone National park
50. Visit 30 national parks and geocache along the way
51. Ride a mule down the Grand Canyon
52. Visit Mammoth Cave in Kentucky
53. Visit Mount Rushmore

54. Hike the Appalachian Trail
55. Hike through the petrified Forest national Park in Arizona
56. Visit Niagara Falls
57. Tour of Hoover dam
58. Visit the White House
59. Visit Ellis Island
60. Visit the Alamo
61. Visit Ground Zero in New York
62. Ring in the new year in Times Square
63. Go ice skating at Rockefeller Center
64. Visit the Biltmore
65. Attend the Rose Parade
66. Attend the Macy's Thanksgiving Day Parade
67. Renew your wedding vows in Las Vegas
68. Drive to palm beach in a convertible
69. Visit Disneyland with kids
70. Go to Disney World without children

71. Witness the rocket launch at Cape Canaveral
72. Attend San Diego's comic con
73. Attend a taping of Saturday Night Live
74. See a Broadway show
75. Attend a concert at Carnegie Hall
76. Attend the Boston Pops
77. Visit the grand old operate
78. Visit Graceland, the home of Elvis
79. Visit the rock 'n roll Hall of Fame and Museum in Cleveland
80. Attend an opera
81. Attend a performance of Cirque du Soleil
82. Visit the Alps in Europe
83. Tour 20 castles in Europe
84. Drink beer at Oktoberfest in Munich
85. Drive the Audubon
86. Visit the tulips in Holland
87. Visit the Eiffel Tower
88. Attend the Paris fashion show

89. Visit the Palace of Versailles
90. Attend the Cannes film festival
91. Lay on the sands of the French Riviera
92. See the cave paintings in France
93. Take a trip on the Orient express
94. Take the Chunnel from English into France
95. See the changing of the guard at Buckingham Palace
96. See big Ben
97. Attend a service at Westminster Abbey
98. Visit Oxford and Cambridge universities
99. Enjoy a traditional afternoon tea in England
100. Visit Stonehenge
101. Kiss the Blarney Stone
102. See the rock of Gibraltar
103. Visit the Parthenon in Athens
104. Visit the Coliseum
105. Visit the Sistine Chapel

106. Attend Mass by the Pope
107. Ride a gondola in Venice
108. Visit the leaning Tower of Pisa
109. Backpack across Europe
110. See the fjords of Norway
111. Visit Red Square in Moscow
112. Take a boat ride on the Caspian Sea
113. Stand on Masada in Israel
114. See the Dead Sea Scrolls
115. Visit the wailing wall in Jerusalem
116. See the Sea of Galilee
117. Visit the pyramids in Giza, Egypt
118. See the great Sphinx of Giza
119. Visit the Sahara desert
120. Go on a photographic safari to Africa
121. Publish a book of your photographs in Africa
122. See the grandeur of Victoria Falls
123. Visit the Taj Mahal
124. See Mount Everest, the world's highest mountain

125. See China's terra-cotta Warriors
126. Hike the Great Wall of China
127. Participate in a Japanese tea ceremony
128. Ride the bullet train by Mount Fuji
129. Visit the Hiroshima peace Memorial Park
130. Visit the country of your ancestors
131. Visit all seven continents
132. Visit the North Pole
133. Visit the South Pole
134. Take a round the world cruise
135. Collect sea shells on a foreign beach
136. SCUBA dive in the great barrier reef
137. Climb the Sydney Harbour Bridge
138. Go on a walk about in Australia
139. Visit Easter Island
140. Snorkel in the Caribbean
141. Cruise the Panama Canal
142. Visit some Mayan ruins
143. Cruise the Amazon River
144. Visit the Galapagos Islands

145. Visit Machu Picchu
146. See Christ the Redeemer statue in Rio de Janeiro
147. Attend Carnival in Rio de Janeiro
148. Watch soccer in Brazil
149. Take a horse-drawn carriage ride
150. Ride an elephant
151. Ride a camel
152. Swim with the dolphins
153. Go whale watching
154. Go shark diving
155. See polar bears in their natural environment
156. See penguins in their natural habitats
157. Visit an alligator farm
158. Visit the USS Arizona Memorial in Hawaii
159. Visit the World War II Memorial in Washington DC
160. Visit the American Cemetery and Memorial in Normandy France

161. Visit the American Cemetery of the Battle of the Bulge in Brussels Belgium
162. Visit a Nazi concentration camp
163. Embark upon an epic animal adventure
164. Take the ultimate themed road trip

Technology

165. Learn social media
166. Attempt to become Internet famous
167. Become proficient in a new computer skill
168. Become certified in a new computer skill

Sports and Fitness

169. Learn to snow ski
170. Learn to water ski
171. Go heli-skiing
172. Go tubing down a lazy river
173. Go kayaking

174. Paddle a canoe
175. Ride cross-country on a bicycle
176. Ride a bicycle built for two
177. Ride a motorcycle
178. Run a marathon on all seven continents
179. Wade in a cranberry bog
180. Get in shape
181. Lose 80 pounds
182. Face your greatest fear
183. Coach a local sports team
184. Take up kick boxing
185. Join a Crossfit Gym
186. Learn to fence
187. Learn to play racquetball
188. Attend the Olympics
189. Attend a major tennis tournament
190. Attend a major golf tournament
191. Adopt a stretch of highway through the adopt a highway program
192. Tour wineries in Napa Valley

193. Bicycle across the US
194. Go horseback riding down the Grand Canyon
195. Run a marathon
196. Run a half marathon
197. Ride a horse on the beach
198. Tour an aircraft carrier
199. Visit the tomb of the unknown soldier at Arlington national Cemetery
200. Visit a place totally out of your element
201. Try an extreme sport
202. Have bariatric sleeve surgery
203. Bungee jump

Spiritual

204. Write an unexpected letter to a friend
205. Write a poem
206. Memorize an entire chapter in the Bible
207. Prepare and give a sermon
208. Learn to meditate

209. Visit an ashram in India

Social/Food related

210. Learn to ballroom dance
211. Create a signature dish
212. Make potato chips for your next party
213. Enter a pie eating contest
214. Make bread from scratch
215. Roast chestnuts over an open fire
216. Pull taffy
217. Eat ice cream for breakfast
218. Plan a garden and grow your own produce
219. Share a secret recipe with a friend
220. Host a 60s party
221. Host a 70s party
222. Meet your favorite celebrity
223. Be a celebrity for a day
224. Try out for a reality show
225. Make your own wine
226. Create your own unique beverage

227. Make your own beer
228. Eat the most memorable meal imaginable
229. Try an exotic food
230. Do an ultimate friends weekend
231. Run a billboard thanking someone for a month
232. Mentor the local dentist on growing his business
233. Organize a pamper day for your friends
234. Pick your friends up in a stretch limo
235. Design and develop your own signature cocktail
236. Commit to a new diet for a month
237. Become the ultimate movie buff

Out of the ordinary

238. Ride in a glass bottom boat
239. Take a helicopter ride
240. Take a hot air balloon ride

241. Ride in a blimp
242. Fight in a jet fighter
243. Go skydiving
244. Go hang gliding
245. Ride a zip line
246. Go bungee jumping
247. Ride one of the world's fastest roller coasters
248. Ride a mechanical bull
249. Attend a stranger's funeral
250. Climb a tree
251. Build a treehouse
252. Learn a foreign language
253. Take a night class just for fun
254. Conquer your biggest fear
255. Live out your favorite scene from your favorite movie
256. Become a janitor for the day at a local private school
257. Experience your ultimate water adventure

258. Experience what it's like to live during your favorite time.
259. Learn how to defend yourself
260. Make a summer reading list
261. Building an ant farm
262. Become a rescue center for homeless dogs and cats
263. Attend a serious dog or cat show
264. Show your dog at one of these shows
265. Record a World War II veterans memories of his/her experiences
266. Live in a foreign country for six months
267. Invent something
268. Start a collection
269. Build a giant sand castle on the beach
270. Paint a picture good enough to hang on your wall
271. Build a model airplane or ship
272. Building dollhouse from scratch
273. Build a piece of furniture

274. Make your log sculpture with a chainsaw
275. Write to your favorite living author and tell this author why you enjoy his or her work
276. Write a letter to a company whose products you like
277. Volunteer on a political campaign
278. Memorize the preamble to the Constitution
279. Memorize the Gettysburg Address
280. Buy a membership to your local museum
281. Become a docent at a local museum
282. Create a model train display
283. Memorize the names of all the presidents in order
284. Have a star named after you
285. Have your portrait painted
286. Memorize a favorite poem
287. Learn to speed read

288. Learn sign language
289. Take a cooking class
290. Take a first aid class
291. Learn CPR
292. Drive a Formula One car
293. Go to chef school
294. Go to clown college
295. Learn one or two truly impressive magic tricks
296. Watch every James Bond movie
297. Try out for a part in a theater production
298. Join a book club
299. Make a list of all the books you wanted to read
300. Write a children's book
301. Compose a song
302. Learn to play the bagpipes
303. Learn to play the harmonica

304. Become especially well read and something totally outside what you've done in the past
305. Pioneer a fashion trend
306. Fill your office with children's toys and play with them
307. Teach a class at your local community college on something you know a lot about
308. Organize a rally or an event for something that matters to you
309. Perform an amazing favor for a stranger
310. Attempt to crash or sneak into an event
311. Emcee an event
312. Set up a woodworking shop and design furniture
313. Write the best, most meaningful, most compelling letter you've ever written to your children

314. Engage in some sort of secret spy activity
315. Get on TV
316. Dress like somebody famous
317. Tell an epic life to a stranger
318. Destroy something
319. Witness one of nature's most rarely occurring events
320. Make up your very own superhero personified
321. Make a dramatic change in your appearance
322. Do something that totally transcends your current age
323. Create a screenplay and submit it to a Hollywood producer

Family/Legacy

324. Start a new family tradition
325. Visit a relative you've never met in any foreign country

326. Visit a relative you've never met in this country
327. Take up genealogy
328. Give a toast at a wedding
329. Find your best friend from grammar school
330. Write your life story in a book
331. Return to your childhood home and ask for a tour
332. Watch reruns of a television show you loved as a kid
333. Attend your class reunion
334. Make contact with a high school classmate you haven't seen since graduation
335. Write a personal mission statement
336. Make and bury a time capsule
337. Break a bad habit
338. Asked for forgiveness from someone you've hurt

339. Forgive someone who has wronged you
340. Turn an enemy into a friend
341. Be kind to a stranger
342. Give a surprise gift to that special person in your life
343. Confront a past embarrassment
344. Plan your next class reunion